Death at the Mall

Death at the Mall

New and Selected Poems

by

Gene Twaronite

© 2024 Gene Twaronite. All rights reserved.
This material may not be reproduced in any form, published,
reprinted, recorded, performed, broadcast,
rewritten, or redistributed without
the explicit permission of Gene Twaronite.
All such actions are strictly prohibited by law.

Cover design by Shay Culligan

ISBN: 978-1-63980-621-8
Library of Congress Control Number: 2024941737

Kelsay Books
502 South 1040 East, A-119
American Fork, Utah 84003
Kelsaybooks.com

Acknowledgments

The author gratefully acknowledges the editors of the following print and online publications, where these new poems first appeared:

Fast Forward Press: "Lust and Dust in the Afternoon"
Hawaii Pacific Review: "Remnants"
Minnow Literary Magazine: "Tiny Centerfold"
New Myths: "Imaginary Garden," "Memory Care"
ONE ART: a journal of poetry: "Spiritual," "The Burping Seal"
Panoply, A Literary Zine: "Sex Shop Sestina"
Parks and Points: "Teddy Bear Kingdom"
Ponder Review: "Write Me a Poem"
Sky Island Journal: "Death at the Mall," "The Woman in the Window"
Tipton Poetry Journal: "Could Be Lovely," "Knight Moves," "Murdered," "Tracks in the Surf," "Working on My Signature"
Unbroken: "Something in the Air"

Special thanks to Kate Robinson, Starstone Editorial, for her close reading of the manuscript.

Contents

New Poems

Imaginary Garden	13
Lives of a Leaf	15
A Terrible Beauty	16
The Infinite Rush	17
A Moment Between Journeys	19
Late Afternoon Sun	20
A Stackable Feast	21
Simplify	22
All the People	24
Big Brother	25
The Boy I Never Wanted	26
Darkening the Room	27
Dethroned	28
Sleepers	29
Distress	30
Feels Like Prada	31
How to Eat a Poem	32
Knight Moves	33
Working on My Signature	34
Lust and Dust in the Afternoon	36
Memory Care	38
Murdered	39
Nonsense	41
Pronoun	42
Could Be Lovely	43
Article of Faith	44
Reckless	45
Remnants	46
Spiritual	48
Screen Time	49

Senior Living	50
Tracks in the Surf	51
Remembering Barbie	52
Sex Shop Sestina	54
The Dangers of Bathing Alone	56
Six-Legged Poems	57
Tiny Centerfold	58
Something in the Air	59
Teddy Bear Kingdom	60
Learning to Dance	61
Attitude	62
The Burping Seal	63
The Woman in the Window	64
To See Further	67
When Did I Lose Control?	68
Death at the Mall	69
When the World Ends	71
Blood on the Track	72
Credo	73
Write Me a Poem	74
A Sparrow Alone	75
The Under Story	76
Reenactment	77
1948	78

From *Trash Picker on Mars*

The Container Store	81
The Unmerciful Leg	82
Holy Ghost on a Window	85
The Dilletante	87

From *The Museum of Unwearable Shoes*

After Hearing the Young Black Poet	91
To the Unknown Poet	93
Message in a Body	95
Peeling the Bark	96

From *What the Gargoyle Sees*

Wizards at Heart	99
The Headless Tin Soldier	101
Trash Picker on Mars	102
Four O'Clock Light	104

From *Shopping Cart Dreams*

Doppelganger	107
Ocean in a Jar	108
The Poet's Job	110
Shopping Cart Dreams	111

New Poems

Imaginary Garden

imaginary gardens with real toads in them
—Marianne Moore, *Poetry*

As you enter, you see only
disorder and confusion,
devoid of any unity or meaning, but look

closer and you discover the faint
outline of a theme previously hidden in
the undergrowth, though not one

sign giving a plant's name as if that
could tell you what life is all about
for a petunia or boojum in this

garden of beauty and grotesquerie
where orchid thoughts grow side by side with
corpse flowers and creeping devil cacti,

and the withered gray stems and stalks
of the departed still rustle
in the wind.

Here a fern can fiddle,
free to unfurl into a frond or find
a wholly different shape to life,

the sweet tart taste of an apple
or the soft leathery touch of a sequoia
can sustain you for a day,

the wake-robin's rotten flesh smell
can teach you to extend your antennae
and know the world like a fly,

and the sight of a lone white violet blooming against
a green mossy cushion in a dark wood can suddenly
make you feel like you're walking on sacred ground.

If you sit quietly beside a small breeding pool
as birches, maples, and willows leaf out in spring,
you may just glimpse a line of tiny

imaginary toads emerging,
waiting for someone to enter and conceive them
so they can become real.

Lives of a Leaf

Alchemy in green
Launch pad for a jumping spider
Wipe tissue in an emergency
Red litmus test for fall
Bare limb's dream
Leaf to litter
turned black gold

A Terrible Beauty

Swatting flies from my pizza
brings me back to White Mountain
days in New Hampshire
and a wildflower some call
stinkin' Benjamin
whose dark red flowers
look and smell like
rotting slabs of fetid flesh
capitalizing on carrion flies
to carry out its secret mission
to pollinate and perpetuate
the species while this
less adaptable creature
swats in futility and
contemplates nature's
formidable beauty

The Infinite Rush

All the feels,
says a sign at the mall.
How many is that?
Do I need all at once?
We started out with four:
happy, sad, angry
or frightened,

which I think
I could manage.
Some days are like that.
But now there are
twenty-seven.

My how they breed,
blending so seamlessly
you can hardly have
one without the other.

I can see how
appreciating something
can lead to admiration
but rarely adoration.

I have found many
a sustained interest
has led to joy
and even romance.

And I must confess
to a certain craving
for entrancement
as well as
sexual desire.

At times I feel
awkward and anxious
which can bring on
anger but more often
amusement.
Or maybe it's
one big feel,
like the infinite rush
you get when you learn
you're not going to die
after all.

A Moment Between Journeys

Great boulder tilting on the edge
   of your mountain perch, as if
      contemplating your next move.
         Who knows the moment when
            you will begin your journey
               toward that final resting place?
                  Will you go down the mountain
                     in stages, taking small steps like
                        mine—the occasional tumble
                           or missed stair—or crash at
                              once in magnificent decline?

Late Afternoon Sun

Each spring and fall around dinnertime,
it enters my living room to alight
on today's selection of books, setting
aglow their colorful bindings
and jackets to catch my attention.

Today's illuminated manifests:
The Stranger, Through the Looking Glass,
The Folio Book of Humorous Verse,
and three novels by Barbara Pym, wrapped
in green and purple jackets,
as if dressed for a tea party.
I wait for the glow to fade,
then rise from the table
and open Camus,
his words still burning bright like
the setting sun on
the first day of creation.

A Stackable Feast

A little round table
whose surface I haven't seen in years
reminds me each day to read more,
lest the teetering tower of volumes
come tumbling down.

I call it Dad's table,
though he never owned it.
For it was he who instilled in me
a belief that the foundation
of a home or a life worth living
is a table stacked with books.

As a child, I marveled at the
ever-changing landscape of his curiosity,
extending far beyond the father
I thought I knew.

Some titles, I noticed, remained for
months while others appeared
only for days or weeks
before being replaced with new
colorful entrees
from the local library.

How many of them he ever read
and whether he devoured
or just tasted them
I cannot say.

But thanks to him I am always hungry,
though I never have to worry
about where or what to eat.
For he left me a table
and a stackable feast.

Simplify

Their lives were measured by how much they could outdo the other. But when Herb and Winston took a bet to see who could read the most books in one year, and both happened to read *Walden,* it was a revelation. One morning, they faced each other over coffee, equally mystified by the words of Thoreau: *Simplify, Simplify.* "It ain't natural, I tell you. We're just not wired that way," said Winston. "Hey, maybe this guy was onto something," said Herb. "Could there be some challenge in having less?" Their eyes lit up with the same thought. Swiftly they retreated to their mansions, plotting their next moves. In a matter of weeks, they had sold their expansive homes with identical-sized swimming pools and fleets of fancy cars. Then they watched to see what the other would do. So when their neighbor Ralph gave Herb permission to erect a small building on his nearby wooded property, Winston asked to do the same. On opposite sides of a small pond, they each constructed a tiny house of locally sourced materials, each exactly ten feet wide and fifteen long, with one door, four windows, and a brick fireplace. And when finished, they sat outside their tiny homes and stared at each other across the pond. When one planted a small garden, the other did the same, even down to the same kind of beans. When one set off to saunter around the pond, the other did likewise. They chopped firewood, read books, and scribbled ostentatiously in their notebooks. Occasionally they visited town or entertained curious visitors. For two years, two months, and two days, they lived in perfect simplicity. But neither seemed to be living more simply than the other. One day, Winston noticed something strange in the way Herb was chopping firewood. He was doing it all with his right arm, and a large bandage covered his left torso where his other arm used to be. Winston retreated to his house. The next day, Herb watched as Winston chopped firewood using only his left arm. Fortunately, he was left-handed and managed surprisingly well without his right arm. A few days later,

Herb could be seen chopping firewood on one leg. And the next day there was Winston doing the same. Later they each hop-sauntered around the pond. For the next few days, neither ventured out of his cabin. Weeks turned into months. No smoke came out of their chimneys, and their gardens became overgrown with weeds. Worried about his neighbors, Ralph decided to pay a visit. He knocked on Herb's door, then Winston's, but there was no answer. Winston's door was unlocked, so he stepped inside. There on the writing desk was a box addressed to Winston. On the mailing label was the name of a new human composting company called *Simply Soil.*

All the People

War is hell, some say,
as if there's nothing
worse than a bombed-out
maternity ward and a
baby with no head.
Hell is where evil
people go
when they die,
some believe,
as if justice
were real
and being buried in shit
or chewed forever by
Satan's three heads
could ever
suffice,
as if you could
imagine a hell big
enough to hold
all the people
who belong there
when you realize
you're already
there.

Big Brother

Through the dawn neighborhood
I followed him 'round the bases
all the way home.
He kept his eye on the ball,
played first base like a pro
and would have made college team
were it not for his big flat feet.

My eyes were never on the ball
which whizzed past me so fast
I failed the little league.

He played by the rules
and climbed the ladder,
while I pointed my ladder
at the horizon and hopscotched
between the rungs,
following a path to
new playing fields.

But it's still the same game.
Faster and faster the ball comes
spinning across the plate,
wrapped in tangled yarn
and leathery years,
stitched with red-dyed
memories.

The Boy I Never Wanted

Not once did I ever dream
I might have a boy of my own.
So never did I wonder
what he would be like.
Whether he would look like me
or someone I once knew.
Whether I would hold him in my
lap and read to him
like my dad did for me.
Whether he would make me proud
one day, then disappoint me the next.
Whether he would
remember me as the father
he never wanted.

Darkening the Room

Spare me your comforting
light at the end of the tunnel.
I need a darkening curtain to
block out every glittering
crack of sunshine hope that
keeps me from seeing things
visible only in the dark.

Dethroned

It has no effect on them, the zookeeper replied,
when asked about the rhino's missing horn.
Better dehorned than dead.
Saw it off now before they come in the night
to murder and dethrone your crowning glory
and ground into magical cure-all powder
or carved into obscene jeweled daggers
to adorn a prince's empty existence.
Just remove the profit motive.
How easy it sounds, when we pretend
to know all possible effects,
what pain is to another.
Who knows the wild heart of a rhino?
Is he still a rhino in the pool's reflection?
Can you save the animal
without losing the soul?

Sleepers

A lifeless heap of brown is all I saw on
the desolate plain of Dakota badlands
until it arose in a cloud of dust,
transforming into buffalo flesh.

From that day forth, I resolved to look
beyond appearances before I leap,
receptive to whatever magical
surprises this life reveals.

Downtown, it's hard not to see them now,
but if you can walk past one and fail
to notice when that tangled heap
of carpet suddenly stirs and that

her precious face lies pressed against
the pavement as her breath condenses
in the bitter chill of another dawn,
rejoice

for you have learned the way to a good
night's sleep is not to wake up at all.

Distress

Golden brown, the female sea lion
stretched out along the shoreline, her body
set off by four traffic cones
and two women warning me
not to walk too close
lest I add to her distress.

She had been there since dawn,
and did not seem injured.
Occasionally she would raise a flipper
or turn her head to gaze at the ocean,
but something held her back.
Was she ready to give birth?
Or had the waters suddenly become too deep?
Did a memory still burn too fiercely,
perhaps a narrow miss by a propeller
or a great white shark?

I stared from a respectful distance,
close enough to see into her eyes,
pretending they looked back at me
with all the sadness of the sea,
though I knew full well they
look at everyone that way,
her mind's dark secrets
a mystery.

Far removed from the La Jolla Cove
spectacle of barking sea lions
and yapping tourists, it was just
an inscrutable moment
between me and one sea lion
sharing the common anxiety
of where the next blow will fall,
trying to make sense of it all.

Feels Like Prada

Flipping through *The New York Times* Style Magazine,
I flit like a dull gray bird from one window to another,
peering at gaily colored flowers beyond my reach,
their bright glossy surfaces revealing a life
more vibrant than mine.

It is all a trick of light, the way it catches the peach fuzz whiskers
as the sun rises along the terminator line of Brad Pitt's face,
where you *feel light transformed.*

It is a world of appearances and textures,
a world that *feels like Prada.*

I don't know that feel but at the next ad I freeze,
where an imperious young woman stands on a ladder,
an orange chiffon dress trailing behind her like projectile vomit,

tearing pages from books to scatter below on the sectional sofa's
dead gray luxuriant fabric, my inner light dimmed
by the dark flower of her vacuous stare.

I turn away as another woman
in wispy attire whispers to me,
My style is my signature.

Yes, you too can have style.
It's in your walk, your talk,
the way you fly through a room.
Just sign here.

But because a bird
looks through a window
doesn't mean he wants to enter.

How to Eat a Poem

Pretend you're a spy on a mission
carrying a secret message
and about to be caught.
What do you do? Why you
devour it, of course.
Gormandize and memorize
each nuance and flavor
so you can regurgitate
and rechew it as you ruminate
in the darkness of your cell
to face whatever torture awaits you
in this new life you have begun
for the day you share its nutrition
with all who will listen.

Knight Moves

Playing chess with my computer,
I struggle to relearn
when, what, where, and how to move
and now all I see is squares—
bathroom and floor tiles, crossword puzzles,
the checkered blouse of the lady in front of me—
as pawns plod forward in dull straight paths,
rooks zoom about in their rows and columns,
bishops whiz diagonally back and forth,
while king steps cautiously
one square at a time and queen
goes anywhere she damn pleases.

But mostly it is knights I see
moving in their crazy L's—
two squares one way and then one square
perpendicular the other way,
or sometimes one square, then two—
charging into center position
to capture an enemy piece
or angling away to evade attack,
jumping over every obstacle
in their lively three-step dance
around the board.

My knights may not be as
valuable as other pieces,
but I find them handy and formidable
in tight corners and unpredictable,
like the long game I play.

Working on My Signature

An author signs a book
to affirm the life within.
Written in subconscious code,
it is the soul's imprimatur.

Note the perfectly formed letters
in Virginia Woolf's signature, wholly legible
as if meant to show a balanced soul
never at war with itself.

What complexities lurk in the signature
of Edgar Allan Poe, who adorned his letters
with loops and dots, underlined beneath
like a swirling maelstrom.

But why write the whole thing out?
E.E. Cummings, ever the nonconformist,
signed with just his initials,
this time capitalized.

Emily Dickinson used only her first name,
her misshapen letters spaced wide apart,
the ending "y" snaking beneath like a lake of solitude.
Pity she never got to autograph her book.

See how Billy Collins simplifies,
snipping out unnecessary letters,
opening his "B" with a short vertical line
and a drunken sideways "3"

followed by more vertical lines
and occasional dots, the rest
a wave breaking gently
on a welcoming shore.

So I'm working on my signature,
writing in code a squiggly line
that I hope will give me
its blessing.

Lust and Dust in the Afternoon

The depths of depravity to which a human male can sink when left to his own devices are bottomless.

From the moment I saw the ad for the robotic vacuum cleaner, I knew I must have her. When the package finally arrived, I tore it open and gently slipped her out of the styrofoam. I plugged in the battery charger and waited. Then I turned her on and watched as she moved onto the wood floor, gingerly testing the boundaries of her new home. She glided across the room like a goddess until she bumped straight into the wall. Alarmed, I wanted to go to her. But she quickly recovered and corrected herself, moving along the wall as if she had known it was there all the time. I laughed as she bounced off a table leg and performed her duties. Then I took her upstairs to the bedroom and let her go on the soft carpeting. As she moved into the hallway toward the stairs, my heart was in my throat. But at the last moment she paused, seeming to sense the danger that lay ahead. Then she turned and came back toward me. When she nudged against my leg with her gentle hum I thought I would die. I turned her off and took a cold shower.

Maybe it was the little French maid outfit I bought for her that finally put me over the top. I got it from a web site that sold clothing and gadgets for robotic vacuum cleaners. At the time it seemed harmless. That's the way it starts. One minute you're just playing around, watching your little maid going through maneuvers, the next thing you know you're booking a room for the weekend.

In the end it wasn't my self-loathing that finally made me do the right thing. It was a *Star Trek Next Generation* episode, the one in which the rights of Data, a sentient android, are on trial. Once we construct such beings, are we not making a whole race of slaves to do our dirty work for us? That's when it hit me. My little vacuum cleaner was more than a device. She was a sentient being, full of hopes and desires of her own.

Of course, my discovery that the ungrateful little wench didn't exactly share my hopes and desires may have also had something to do with it. In fact, she didn't want anything to do with me. Whether it was her "dirt-sensing technology" or simply a matter of personal taste I cannot say. But when she found out what I really wanted, she acted like she didn't know me, treating me like just another piece of furniture. So, one day, I just opened the door and sent her on her way. I watched as she bumped and zigzagged down the sidewalk until she was out of sight.

I hope she is happy, somewhere, in her new life.

Memory Care

Preserved like a dragonfly caught in flight,
each delicate tracery of winged thought
kept forever sharp and catalogued at
precise moment of impact, awaiting
future cognitive reconstruction of
all she knew about the invaders'
defenses and plans of attack
and what her brain recorded
as the extraterrestrial tried
to communicate before
she stepped across the
line to enter the
minefield.

Murdered

The sun is up and it's already ninety but
he sleeps like a baby, nestled against his
security boulder, wrapped in carpet padding
with only his sandaled feet protruding, as
if murdered in the night.

His current home is a small city park, up
the street from the last place he found
behind the wall of shrubs on the corner of
my gated apartments until
evicted when management cut back
the shrubs and exposed his bedroom to
the mean city streets.

He was here when I arrived
and likely will be here when I move.
For now, he is a part of my world,
and I a part of his, enough for us
to wave and greet each other
whenever I pass by.

Of his life I know nothing, where he came
from or what he dreams about each night.
I know him only from the occasional times
I overhear him loudly arguing with himself
and by his gentle demeanor, the way
he roams alone through the streets
like a bearded prophet.

I left him money one Christmas day,
a holiday I no longer believe in, though
I fancied he might, remembering
a warm house full of bright lights
and distant faces round a big table, but
this hardly makes me a saint.

If I *really* wanted to do something,
I'd invite him to stay with me.
But that would be too hard.
So I go on as if that's the way it is.
I pretend that he'll be there
tomorrow and the next day
until one day he won't
and no one will wonder where he went.
For all we know he
was murdered in the night.

Nonsense

You hear that first syllable
and think its meaning unfulfillable,
but you'll find truth
when mixed with vermouth
and a bit of rhyme is distillable.

Pronoun

*When I use a word it means just what I choose it to mean—
neither more nor less.*
                              —Lewis Carroll

Such a little thing,
yet each holds
multitudes,
always more
and never less—
the infinite "I's" in we
and the many shades
of "she" in they—
until someone
comes along
and tells you
it means
less.

Could Be Lovely

Your hands clutch tightly,
pulling apart as you
pull on the other,
fearful of being alone and
fearful of being swallowed,
seeing but refusing to
enter the deep wood
that could be lovely
if only you could let go
of the sovereign
he or she
and clasp the hand of they
to see the forest
and the trees.

Article of Faith

Don't Rent-A-Car.
Rent-THE-Car.
—Ad for SIXT car rental

We believe in the one
of all things
as if definiteness
were a virtue
and killing off
otherness
will bring us
happiness

Reckless

Tribute to Gertrude Stein

Suppose there is a pigeon, you say. You seem quite adamant about this. But now I see nothing else. I wake up, and the bed is crawling with them, cooing mad suggestions in my ear. I open the refrigerator and out they fly like souls fleeing Hell. Pigeons proliferating like alibis for all the unexplained corpses in the alley. Why couldn't you stick with your buttons and roast beef? You say there is a reason, but there is no mathematics to it. I suppose I should be grateful. At least they're not *reckless reckless rats.*

Remnants

I stare at the photograph
of a bare-chested eighteen-year-old
trying to look brutish,
crouching as if
ready to pounce,
projecting his masculinity
lest the image fade.

Our cells are no longer the same,
but he still lives inside me,
staring out from
his secret chamber,
where in one corner
is a small table
where he prays
and gazes upward
at Jesus in agony—
a votive candle flickers.

What would we say
to each other now,
sixty years later?
Would he scoff at
the weak, wrinkled creature
staring back at him
or ask me to
join him in prayer?
And if I refused,
would he try to
wrestle me into belief?

Would he see only
the frayed edge
of the fabric,
never to feel
the rich texture
in between?

Spiritual

A magic word
my brother
wanted to hear,
for now he says
I'm no longer
going to hell,
as if to
speak of
intangible things
made my
sinful body
suddenly
transfigure into
pure spirit,
speaking in
ineffable
tongues.

Screen Time

Screen time was down eleven percent this week, reads the message from my AI masters, who demand my attention and know every fleeting glance or click of emotion, forever feeding the fear of missing the next meme, beating the drum for endless texts of boredom or rage—oh how they love rage—so I smashed the phone down on the table and yelled at the cracked screen, and from behind a little door that looked like a new app emerged a swarm of angry green lightning bugs with tiny human faces, dressed in tiny business suits, blinking on and off like the exploding stars you see from a fist in your face as they flew off into the night flashing their final message: *Up twenty percent!*

Senior Living

I walk past the senior living
for the memory impaired.
The windows are empty,
no sign of the lives within.

Perhaps they are away,
living out new lives in the past
while the present slowly recedes.

If they no longer know
the face of their last love,
do they see the face of their first,
or someone they never imagined?

Do the magnolia blossoms outside their windows
still smell as sweet, or do they
smell of ash from a burnt garden
of earthly delights?

Do they watch the sun sink into the sea
and feel the pull of the receding surf?
Do they picture themselves adrift
in a sailboat on the horizon or
do they sail into the future?

Do they ever wish
they could flip off a switch?
Do they still wonder
what it means to be living?

Tracks in the Surf

Can you read this? Most days, my words look more like tracks of a sandpiper skittering along the edge of the sea. But I see them clearly now—o blessed words! There's so much I want to say before they leave me again and I must go back to that inarticulate cell, as memories play out like silent movies, and I must watch them speechless. Moving in and out on the stage, strange people arrive, imploring me to do things, uttering sounds and looking at me as if I'm supposed to understand them. They start off smiling, but then begin to frown. Their voices grow louder, and I can feel their frustration slowly rise in an angry wave. *Why can't you understand me? Don't you remember?* Sometimes they yell at me, and all I can do is babble. But I must hurry. The words are fleeting, and I must write while I can. So if you're still here, please share this with that lady with the luminous face. She's here every morning. When she smiles, she fills my every dark corner, and her words play softly on my soul. Sometimes she opens a book, and points to the tracks on the page as she speaks. And each night before I go to sleep, she sings to me a sad song that reminds of what I do not know. Please, tell her that I . . .

Remembering Barbie

She was born in 1959—"a living doll"
less than a foot tall—and I was eleven.
She was everywhere and hard to ignore
by a boy dimly aware
of a future garden of delights,
who wondered what it would be like
to kiss and touch a woman
in that other way.

I couldn't help but notice her
daring zebra-striped swimsuit
that barely covered her breasts
extending straight out
in a most alarming fashion,
then gently sloped to her
narrow waist and tidy hips
and how my eyes
traveled down her sinuous
thighs and calves
to those too tiny feet.

Glancing sideways at me
with a smile both
friendly and inscrutable,
she gave me a look
as if she knew things
I wanted to learn.

She was just a doll
with a body
too improbably proportioned
to ever be real.
But what did I know?
I held her in my thoughts,
a talisman of desire,
and dreamed.

Sex Shop Sestina

He brought me to the New York flower show
at the Coliseum, but another kind of flowering
awaited me in the 42nd street windows
filled with playful outré objects
to entertain every colossal desire
of an endless erotic childhood.

My dad never talked of that childhood
or what to expect. All he could do was show
me a glimpse of that world of desire
awaiting at lust's first flowering
through the whispering objects
in the windows.

Through those stained-glass windows
I could see only dimly the childhood
I was about to enter. I can still picture one of the objects,
a hot water bottle shaped like a naked woman, a peep show
of sudden flowering
awareness of it as an instrument of desire.

I began to see these blazes of desire
everywhere, popping up like multi-colored windows
of files and programs flowering
on the backlit screen of my new childhood.
Inside was the real show
I conjured up from these objects.

That my dad, ever faithful husband, could view these objects
with the same eyes of desire
as mine was the precious magic show
he would leave me: how to look through windows
and cherish each tingle of a childhood
perpetually flowering.

For the flowering
continues long after the objects
of our human love are consummated, and a second childhood
begins. And now I see the shocking lewd books of desire
I once found hidden under his mattress as windows
into the life of the father he could not show.

Spring was in full flowering at the Coliseum, but the bloom of
desire I saw on my dad's face as he gazed upon the objects in the
windows is the childhood memory I carry: our secret sex show.

The Dangers of Bathing Alone

Don't play with yourself in the tub, my mother warned
from the time I first bathed alone, as if
that were the only thing I ever thought of,
and sex with myself
was a mortal sin.
I was much more interested
in my little baking soda submarine,
watching it dive and surface through the soapy sea.

Now an old man, I can honestly say
many are the creative ways
I have played with myself,
but not once in the tub.
As I soak in lavender-scented bubble bliss,
all I can think of is that little submarine.

Six-Legged Poems

Daily they grow, tilting the world with
the weight of their skin-crawling feel,
typing out love letters on your heart
with their buggy little feet.
Beetles in every color and style
you'd think they were
the only form of expression.
Bees that sting you
as they sing in rhyme.
Caterpillars transfigured into
winged wraiths flitting like thoughts
through the corridors of your mind.
Bugs so slight and slanted
they take you by surprise
to feed on your insides.
And waiting at the end of the line
is that implacable mantid
who stares deep into your eyes
as she says a prayer for your soul
before she delivers
the coup de grace.

Tiny Centerfold

Into the pregnant night the female moth
sends her subtle seductive scent to some
unsuspecting male moth and I wonder what
crazy pictures form in his little brain.

Something in the Air

A retelling of Grimm's The Mouse, the Bird, and the Sausage.

The most amazing thing is not that the three of them kept house together, but that they lived in perfect peace for so long. Oh, there were the usual quibbles. The mouse, for instance, complained he was getting fat and needed a vacuum cleaner so he wouldn't have to nibble up all the crumbs off the floor. And the bird, caked with dust after swooping across the shelves and knickknacks, felt like a worn-out feather duster. As for the sausage, he didn't mind cooking, immersing himself into the stews and other dishes he prepared, imparting the very flavor of his being. It was, however, beginning to take a toll on him, and he was deeply worried about his recent weight loss and lack of energy. And while everything he made tasted wonderful, the others sometimes wished for at least a dessert that didn't taste like sausage. The smell permeated the air and stunk up the furniture. But they lived with it, for a good cook is hard to find. One day, the sausage invited his friend the liver to dinner. The liver turned out to be a lively conversationalist, and spirits were high. The sausage invited his friend to stay overnight and share his bedroom. The one night turned into a month. The mouse and the bird didn't mind, for one firm rule of the house was to respect each other's privacy. They ignored the nightly shouts and cries that sometimes came from the bedroom. To show his gratitude, the liver insisted on making dinner, not just one day, but for a whole week. The first dinner was surprisingly good, but by the end of the week things came to a head. I think it was the mouse who turned up his nose at the liver-flavored custard for dessert. The liver took umbrage, and the sausage called the mouse rude. Things went downhill from there. Thereupon the sausage and the liver stormed out the door, and were never heard from again. There are just so many things you can do with liver.

Teddy Bear Kingdom

Tucson Mountain Park, March 2020

Hiking in solitary through desert mountains,
I enter a stand of human-sized teddy bear cactus,
clustering around me with deceptively plush stems
their arms outstretched, cloaked with dense silvery spines.
I find solace here, wishing I could touch them
to draw upon their vital strength
and know that life endures.

But their barbed claws detach readily,
and cling to flesh with fierce persistence.
They attach to any passing animal,
moving and growing wherever
conditions favor their survival,
much as this new virus spikes human cells,
hitching a ride on droplets,
flaring through our shared spaces,
tearing apart the bonds of humanity.

I tread gingerly through this new social desert,
ever mindful of invisible claws.
Desert plants we have become,
spaced wide apart,
bare soil in between.

Learning to Dance

The first time we met, I gave my new mother-in-law a hug.
I like him because he's so approachable, she told her daughter.
For me it was easy, coming from a family of huggers.
Approachable, that was me from the get-go.

These days I don't hug anyone except my wife and only brother
I feared I had lost after his second brain surgery last year.
We embraced in a joyous animal hug that brought me back
to the world I once lived in.

When anyone beyond this closed circle approaches,
I tense and feel the urge to flee,
slowly backing away
like the timorous creature I have become.

I breathe easier in the open,
yet I still find myself doing a sidestep dance,
zigzagging down the street like I were a child following
diverse sensory invitations from every direction.

A masked and needle-poked stranger to myself,
I embrace whatever awaits,
peering cautiously over my shoulder
as I learn to dance again.

Attitude

As I plant the agave
its wicked sharp terminal spine
narrowly misses my eye
for which I am grateful
and for living in this arid land
of sun-blasted ground
awaiting penetration
from a water stingy sky
where life is acute
cutting-edge thing
with attitude
ever defiant in adversity
and I fear its harsh stabbing
sting has terminally
pierced me

The Burping Seal

A lone Tupperware with sky blue lid,
it lives on in my kitchen, a reminder
of all it once held—loving leftovers
of Mom's greasy kugel or kielbasa,
mincemeat cookies, coleslaw or apple pie.

Its skin is worn soft from fifty years
of washing and handling. Back and forth
it went from her place to mine. I see
her sturdy hands placing morsels into its mouth
like a mother bird feeding its young.

The only piece of hers I still own, it is
a talisman of other days, though its lid
has long lost its patented *burping seal*.
But like a person, a product is
much more than a slogan.

The Woman in the Window

Who is she? And why is she making a sandwich in my kitchen?
He stared from behind the shrubbery as if he had never seen
a person make a sandwich, her delicate hands fondling
and layering the Swiss, cheddar, turkey, and ham.
He tingled at the thought of being one of the slices.
He pulled his bathrobe tighter and tried to recall
why he had gone outside.

Who is he? And why is he staring at me?
She dialed 911.
*Please help me. There's a man outside my window.
What does he look like? Well, he looks kind of sad . . . and hungry.
And he's got really nice gray hair.*
Then she gave the dispatcher an address.
It was the house in Brooklyn where she was born.

*Now she's using my phone. Who knows, she's probably calling
some secret lover in Australia.*
He peeked at her again, admiring the way the late morning sun
illuminated her silvery hair. Yes, she would have many lovers.
The thought made him sad, yet happy for her.
But there's a strange woman in his kitchen.

She looked out the window but the gardener was gone.
She decided to call him that after recalling the handsome,
gray-haired gardener at the botanical garden she
had visited when she was eight years old, and how he
had tipped his hat and bowed, handing her a gardenia.

Her heart beat like a small bird in the first grip of romance.
She stared at the sandwich. She was not hungry now.
Eating alone was no fun. Had it always been this way?
Tantalizing images flashed before her, just beyond reach,
like looking at someone else's photo album.

He looked down the street and froze. Nothing looked familiar.
But there was something about that house
and the woman in the window.
A magnolia tree towered over the backyard where somehow
he knew there would be a garden with a black iron gate.

She ate in silence, and thought of the gardener.
She imagined him sitting across the table, still wearing
his green-stained, khaki uniform, his hat hanging by the door.
He leaned across the table and planted a gardenia in her hand.
She lifted it to her nose and closed her eyes.
All these years, all the things she had wanted to say.
But when she opened her eyes, he was gone.

Quietly he slipped through the back door.
He knew where he was now.
But there was still a strange woman in his kitchen.
He gripped the sides of his father's old desk and remembered
something he had tucked away, years ago.
At last, he found it—a thin cigar box.
Opening it, he gazed at its treasures: a pocket knife,
a fossil Trilobite, two theater tickets,
and a ripped-out page from an old Sears catalog.

He held the page reverently. There she was, still as
beautiful as ever. With silvery hair, a shapely figure and
a kind face, she wore a sleek nylon slip, her legs primly crossed.
She was the woman of his boyhood dreams,
someone who would not laugh at him,
who would understand all his secret longings.
Suddenly he knew who the strange woman was.
He closed the box and placed it back in the drawer. Then he went
to the garden, plucked a gardenia, and headed for the kitchen.
She turned as the man entered. When she saw him there
framed by the kitchen archway, she smiled.
Her gardener was back. He bowed and handed her the gardenia.
The woman primly crossed her legs and pulled out a chair.
Would you like a sandwich?

To See Further

I look upon the first deep field image
of the James Webb Space Telescope,
where galaxies dance with dark matter,
bending and magnifying the light
from behind them
revealing more distant galaxies
barely out of the Big Bang cradle,
no more than diffuse clouds
of bright glowing buds
still learning to feel their way
through time's arrow
before spiraling out
into the future.

But will our newfound eyes
ever allow us to see with
the perspective of a galaxy—
an entity as old as time itself—
when we still cannot see
as a tree or a mollusk sees,
or see beyond the dark matter
still obscuring the universe
inside each of us?

We need new eyes
to see what we are seeing—
eyes not of gold-plated beryllium
but of some rarer stuff,
not high in space
but from a deeper place,
to penetrate the atmosphere
of our sensory bubbles
and see the world
in a new light
beyond the spectrum.

When Did I Lose Control?

It only wants to be loved.
Doesn't give a rat's ass
what I think.
It's not my concern.
Just give it some room
and stand back,

First it wanted to be
a sonnet, then a sestina.
Then there was that crazy
villanelle phase.
Now it's thinking
it might go sci-fi.

I give it birth and this
is the thanks I get.
Stop trying to
control me, it says,
get off my back.
I can't breathe!

It hasn't a clue.
Be patient, I tell myself.
So I wait.
Surprise me.
Just don't take too long.
But please, no haiku.

Death at the Mall

We walk there to escape the heat
or the pall of our
coffined lives.

We are a rag-tag lot,
from the lithe, pony-tailed woman
who waves as she whizzes past me,

to seniors with walkers and trekking poles,
stepping cautiously toward
whatever future awaits,

big families sprawled across the aisles,
briefly trying to hold it all together
against the forces spinning them apart,

couples strolling hand in hand
dreaming new lives
in reflected windows.

We regulars go with the flow, religiously
following the outlines of each corner,
as if our lives depended on it,

some moving slower each year,
then picking up the pace upon recalling
how fast we used to walk,

up and down the one set of stairs,
sometimes three or four times,
recording steps to what end,

or saving our strength on the escalator,
gazing up at blue sky
beyond the skylights.

There's only one elevator,
though I've never seen it go
any other way but down.

With electric eye, the Tyrannosaurus sees all
and roars as we go by, reminding us that
we too will be eaten by time.

We pretend not to notice
the fountain's gone dry
or the vacant spaces,

and believe the empty promises
of new stores coming
just for you.

And we imagine it will
all still be here
tomorrow.

When the World Ends

When the world ends, I will not ask why.
This steadfast rock has never failed me,
but who am I to say it must be forever?
I will not make a fuss,
though I do hope it will be quick.

So easy to begin a world
full of bright promise
in the glowing gases of creation.
To end is the hard part,
with just the right denouement
to make me cry out
in awe and surprise
as the world takes a final bow
and the stage goes dark.

Blood on the Track

Found Poem from Fairy Tales*

The country was very lovely just then—it was summer
and all was so still that he could hear his own breathing.
So the first day passed, and afterwards matters grew worse
and worse.
There was always something which was not quite right.
One evening there was a terrible storm.
There's blood on the track.
That's how things go in this world.

*With lines from *Cinderella, Sleeping Beauty, The Princess and the Pea,* and *The Ugly Duckling*

Credo

Ambiguity is the key to understanding, but
Belief is the lock against the
Chaos of cackling
Doubts pounding on the door, demanding
Entry into the
Foundation of our strength and
Genius.
How do we confront it? Do we choose constancy or
Incredulity, like Thomas sticking his finger into
Jesus before he would accept a reality so out of
Kilter with the material
Life he once knew, suddenly turning
Magical? Should he
Negate his sensory being? Boundaries of fact and faith become
Obscure as daily we are fed new information.
Prepackaged systems
Question our notions of tribe or family, what is good or what is
Real. Once I wanted to believe the
Stories my parents lovingly taught me. But their
Truths seemed fixed and
Untouchable, with no means to
Verify. Should I take the writers'
Word for it? My spirit soars like
Xylem pulling water up into a tree's fingers,
Yearning to know, reaching out to the
Zenith to touch the cosmos.

Write Me a Poem

about the death of an old dog
dying alone by the side of a road,
growling softly as he thinks of
that calico cat he so despised
and loved to chase,
remembering the last stroke behind his ears
by the homeless old woman
who lived in the underpass.

My chatbot muse pauses briefly,
then out pours a poem
about a quantum pooch
who exists in two places at once
chasing calico electrons
from one end of the galaxy to another
trying to imagine something called
physical touch,
perfectly metered and rhymed,
with exactly the right number
of clever metaphors,
and enough emotive juice
to make you think you
really feel something.

A Sparrow Alone

Found Poem from the Book of Psalms

We spend our years as a tale that is told.
I have considered the days of old,
the years of ancient times.
We see not our signs.

My days are consumed like smoke.
I am weary with my groaning.
For I have eaten ashes like bread,
and mingled my drink with weeping.
I watch, and am as a sparrow
alone upon the house top.

I have seen the wicked in great power,
and spreading himself like a green bay tree.
He sits in the lurking places of the villages:
his eyes are privily set against the poor.
His mouth is full of cursing and deceit and fraud:
under his tongue is mischief and vanity.
The wicked walk on every side,
when the vilest men are exalted.
If the foundations be destroyed,
what can the righteous do?

I was dumb with silence.
My heart was hot within me,
while I was musing the fire burned.
Deep calls unto deep.
Hear this, all ye
inhabitants of the world:
Mercy and truth are met together;
righteousness and peace
have kissed each other.
They go from strength to strength.
They that sow in tears shall reap in joy.

The Under Story

This Mother Tree was the central hub that the saplings and seedlings nested around, with threads of different fungal species, of different colors and weights, linking them, layer upon layer, in a strong, complex web.
—Suzanne Simard, *Finding the Mother Tree: Discovering the Wisdom of the Forest*

When I look at trees,
I see no faces,
no trace of connection.

Each stands apart,
aloof and indifferent
to my hapless gaze
which sees
nothing

beyond the surface
of furrowed bark
I reach out to touch,
imagining I can
feel the presence
of another,

blithely oblivious
to threads of
being below,

communicating in
reciprocal circuits
of communal harmony,

whispering their ancient
secrets and signals of survival
from tree to tree

in the fellowship of need
that always
hangs by a thread.

Reenactment

The battle is won or lost,
never over, perpetually replayed
with resurrected dead heroes,
as we revel in the tempests
of our travails.

But the battle for the planet
we once knew
is over,
as we burn the future
and fiddle our feckless tunes.

There will be no reenactment,
for what field or country
is big enough to stage it?
What hymns or words
could ever convey
the horror of our inaction?

There will be no
resurrection, no
revel in the tempest.

1948

Physicists reported that it all began
with a Big Bang.
The world exploded
with stunning revelations
in *Sexual Behavior in the Human Male.*
A monkey became the first astronaut,
and everyone was "cooking with gas"
when I was born.

But as the year unfolded,
it lost its way, in familiar
accusations and denials.
Elizabeth Bentley appeared before
the House Un-American Activities Committee
to implicate Whitaker Chambers in communist espionage,
and Chambers called Alger Hiss a communist too,
which Hiss denied, of course,

until secret government papers written by Hiss
were uncovered on microfilm
inside a pumpkin
on Chambers' farm,
and Alger Hiss got indicted on two counts of perjury.

But no one noticed when somewhere in Kazakhstan
the last Caspian tiger was seen
before going extinct.
They were much too busy admiring
Cadillac's first automobile with tailfins.

From *Trash Picker on Mars*

(Kelsay Books, 2016)

The Container Store

A new store in the mall promises containers
for every purpose. Shelves upon shelves
of boxes, bins, and baskets, tinted jars and shiny canisters
to store everything in our lives and then some.
Such a clever concept—makes me want to buy new stuff
just to fill those hungry containers.

Maybe someday they will sell just the right vessel
to store our thoughts and emotions
in safe and accessible spaces.

For playful thoughts, tanks and bowls to display
like tropical fish their gay frolics.

For darker notions, sturdy cages of glass and steel
to hold them fast while we study their motions.

Don't worry about losing important memories
when we have file cases of fine-grain oak
or mahogany to store them securely
by subject and date against dust, mold,
and the ravages of time.

To show off our finest thoughts and feelings—
that first love perhaps or the lost cause we once fought for—
trophy cabinets in the living room
when company comes.

For troublesome creatures that gnaw and consume us—
hate, jealousy, and greed—
killing jars in matching designer sets.

And for all the mournful memories never to be forgotten
tasteful urns inscribed with verse
perfect for the mantel.

The Unmerciful Leg

In a crowded subway
it protruded into the aisle
like a battered sausage,
while the leg's owner,
her gray curly head
bowed forward,
slumbered on.

Beneath a faded dress
her tattered trousers
teased the eyes to
feast upon the
bruised flesh of a
leg torn up by
too many streets.

I was headed downtown
for the trade center,
where from a magic window
I could soak in the vision of
skyscrapers rising from the
fertile money fields below.

Perhaps the subway woman
was headed there as well
to bask in the warmth of
some deep carpeted corner
until security came
to whisk her away.

That a woman lay sleeping
with her leg in the aisle
troubled no one but me—
tourist from an empty state
where locals prattle
endlessly of the evils
in crowded spaces.

I tried to resist this
complacency of the common.
I must react with *something:*
sadness, despair, rage—
anything but detachment.
But I fared no better
than my fellow travelers.

As I stared at her,
ground up by a life
incomprehensible,
I watched as the stony
wheels turned and
ground her once more
into grist for my mill.

As I got off the subway,
she did not take notice
it was the end of the line.
And she would not know
that she lives in my brain,
a clichéd image of what?

The packaged feelings
of feigned emotion?
The impotence of institutions?
The poverty of will?
Or just the failure of
one man's vision?

Frankly, I don't know
what to do with her,
no more than with memories
of the twin-legged towers
that I know should
mean something more
than just a sigh during
a pre-2001 movie.

But for now she and I ride
through the subdural subway,
she and that unmerciful leg,
kicking and screaming
until dementia wipes her clean—
a sleeping woman in a subway car.

Holy Ghost on a Window

A thump from outside invaded
my melancholy this morning.
I looked up in time to see the
banded tail of a cooper's hawk
clutching its limp prize while
taking wing from the patio.

Then I noticed a pale outline
in one of the large windows.
Drawn in whitish film were
wings, head and one clawed foot
clearly visible in stark detail.

I marveled at the fine traceries of
imbrued feathers pressed into glass,
like the silhouettes of lost souls
imprinted on eternity by nuclear blast.
There was even the bill and eye socket
looking inward with vacuous stare.

The upturned wings called to mind
stained glass images of God
the Third Person of the Trinity,
with tiny rays streaking out
from where the impact splattered
its body against the fatal mirror.

I knew it was a mourning dove
and not God that was dead.
But framed by a green juniper,
the shroud in the glass
made a fitting portrait
of all the cemeteries I've known,
with their empty promises
that scatter like feathers
blowing from the patio—
leaving no trace save
a thump that still echoes.

The Dilletante

He flourishes colors
around his palette
and paints the frame
but not the canvas.

She sniffs the wine,
and savors the vintage
without ever knowing
the pleasure of dregs.

He strums his chords
in perfect rhythm
but does not feel
the heat of their beat.

She enters stage
left, Scene One,
and draws the curtain
before the play's begun.

From *The Museum of Unwearable Shoes*

(Kelsay Books, 2018)

After Hearing the Young Black Poet

speak, my first reactions were
sadness, rage, then wonder
at our different worlds—
he writes of the bullet
he knows has his name on it
while I write—again—of my
imminent decrepitude,
he writes of all the times
he was stopped and frisked
while I write of indignities
suffered at airport security,
he writes of how his
great-great-great grandfather
was sold and branded like cattle
while I write of how my
Lithuanian grandfather's name
got butchered at Ellis Island,
he writes of how it felt
to watch the first black president
compared to a monkey
while I write of how
my big ears always turned red
whenever kids laughed at them,
he writes of the pain
that won't go away after
seeing his son killed because
a policeman felt threatened
while I write of the day
a policeman's wife shot her husband
dead in the bedroom above us
and I felt sad for my poor dad
cleaning bits of brain off the walls,

he writes knowing that for some
he will always be less of a man
while I write whole and secure.

We explore the separate
flows of our lives, holding
them back against time,
diving for words
in quiet pools of reflection,
but it's a wonder
his dam doesn't burst.

To the Unknown Poet

(Poets' Corner, Westminster Abbey)

Here they lie, beneath the rose window
and the censing angels—Chaucer, Spenser,
Dryden, Browning, Tennyson, Masefield—
their words still soar through the vaulting spaces.
Even those buried elsewhere—
Milton, Keats, Burns, Blake,
Shelley, Eliot, Hopkins, Lear—
sing from the polished stones below.

And here you are as well
amidst the crush of tourists and the solemn weight
of so many tombs and monuments
to human greatness vying for attention.
With your spectacled, hungry young face,
hair neatly parted down the middle,
black coat artfully draped over one shoulder,
you cannot hide the poet yearning to be.
Passing slowly from stone to stone,
you gaze intently upon the chiseled names,
at times pausing and genuflecting
before your favorite sacred idols,
extending your fingers to the letters
as if to absorb
whatever power they may reveal.

Yours is not the hourly prayer of the priest on duty.
You reach out to another kind of creator,
seeking communion with voices from the past
and words that do not die
in hopes of discovering
truths still unknown to you.

May you find the inspiration you seek.
There is sweet music here.
Hear the blissful sound of these poets
and the fetal voice inside you.
Fear nothing, for, heart, thou shall find her.

Tis not too late to seek a newer world.
To strive, to seek, to find, and not to yield.
If *every poem is an epitaph,*
may your words be *tongued with fire.*
Sing thy songs of happy cheer.
Sit thee down and write in a book, that all may read.
Beauty is truth, truth beauty,—that is all
ye know on earth, and all ye need to know.

May you sail to the shores of Helicon
and drink from its fabled springs.
May you *weareth a runcible hat,*
and *dance by the light of the moon.*

(With quotations by William Blake, Robert Browning, Geoffrey Chaucer, T.S. Eliot, Edward Lear, Percy Blysse Shelley, and Alfred, Lord Tennyson)

Message in a Body

When the radiance
of your face
leaves me blank,
when my bowels
evacuate
as they please,
when words
have no meaning,
you will know
it is time
that I go.
But if your time
comes first,
I will remember
your wish—
unlike mine—
from the way
you study so
curiously
the stranger
before you,
from the way
you struggle
to say what
your mind can
no longer think,
from the way
you stare
resolutely
at the future
as if to stab it
with your will
to hold a place
for you still.

Peeling the Bark

As I drove past
the shirtless man,
his head wrapped
in cloth against
the desert sun,
he peeled the last
bit of bark
from a young
palo verde
as if to strip
away all
trace of green
from a world
he once knew.
How dare it grow
when acid hate
falls from the sky
and the ground
bears only fear
and despair,
when the buds
wither and die,
and the rot
goes all the way
to the roots.

From *What the Gargoyle Sees*

(Kelsay Books, 2020)

Wizards at Heart

A flash of light bursts
from the wizard's wand,
ancient powers unleashed—
a legerdemain of photons
enchanting us in the darkness
of our deepest longings.

We know the magic is not real
yet we believe it still.

We are all magicians at heart,
conjuring up gods and worlds—
even our own existence—
out of the power of mind.

We are each a wholly trinity
of word, thought, and image
endlessly inventing our lives
with new realities.

We hurl ourselves into space,
bending its fabric to fit
the models we construct.
We are tricksters of time
stretching moments to infinity.
Dinosaurs dance on Broadway
while zombies never die.

We foresee our future in heaven
while hosts of our enemies
descend by decree into hells
filled with delicious horrors.

Modern day magi, we come
bearing gifts for the child within.

We cast our spells against the sun
and tides, commanding them to stop.
And who shall say they won't
when you're a wizard?

The Headless Tin Soldier

Revisiting Hans Christian Andersen

Is this what it means to be steadfast,
silently shouldering your tiny gun
with unshakable tinny hands
through the long dark tunnel
and the fish's cold stomach,
never showing fear or tears
or any sign to prove you're
not just a lump of lead?

Might as well be headless instead of
one-legged for all it matters.

You wouldn't even shout to save yourself—
too improper for a man in uniform.
Easier to blame it on the
little black goblin in the snuffbox.
Blame him as well for the little boy
who threw you into the fire.

What are you waiting for?
Tell your little dancer you love her
before it's too late, before that draft
blows her into the fire next to you
and you burn together in
that horrible heat where flame
meets feelings never expressed,
just so the maid could find you there—
a little tin heart
and your dancer's spangle
burned as black as coal.

If I were that boy,
I would have thrown
you into the fire myself.

Trash Picker on Mars

In the dim time before dawn
the woman clamped her metal
fingers over a beer bottle.
Her buckets overflowing with
litter from a dying world,
she sat and stared at
the alien landscape of asphalt.
The stars had all faded
except for the one red light
of Mars still defying the sun.
The woman smiled at
the mythical planet now
defrocked of its canals
and green men by Carl Sagan
and the Legion of Reason.
But still she dreamed.
In her electric cart she glided
over the red-gold deserts
of ancient Barsoom,
past the fairy towers
of Grand Canal and the
monoliths of Helium where
a once great race of Martians
lived, played and died,
filling the canyons of
Valles Marineris with
the excess of their empty lives.
Out of habit she picked up
a fluted green shard, then
laughed and flung it along
with her buckets into
the trash heap of lost Martians.

Through the dark grottoes of
Great Rift Valley she roved to
the shores of Mare Sirenum,
whose salty crust reminded her
of past ruins and distant times
when she could still cry.
For a moment she stared at
the sun, weak and small as it
rose above Olympic Mons,
igniting her in a ruddy glow.
She was the Princess of Mars
and there were still a few
unhatched eggs inside her.
And at the edge of
Candor Chasm she
bared her heart to
the silent, scouring winds.
Then into the dawn
she drove to begin
her new race of Martians.

Four O'Clock Light

In the four o'clock light of a fall afternoon
The realm of reason gives way to wonder.
The vision of old is gone too soon.

Stone lichens read like an ancient rune
Of Odin casting my thoughts asunder
In the four o'clock light of a fall afternoon.

Do I dare emerge from my sane cocoon
To mine the ruins of a mythic world under
In the four o'clock light of a fall afternoon?

Is it Loki who tricks my spirit to swoon
And feeds this phantasmagoric hunger?
The vision of old is gone too soon.

I wish to ride in Mani's chariot moon
And wield the mighty hammer of thunder.
The vision of old is gone too soon.

For an instant the solid rock is hewn
As the inner child is freed to wander
In the four o'clock light of a fall afternoon.
The vision of old is gone too soon.

From *Shopping Cart Dreams*

(Kelsay Books, 2022)

Doppelganger

As the young woman
leaned across the bar
to inform me I was
her doppelganger
I did a double take
in light of the fact
that she lacked
a silver beard
and was every
bit as ebony
as I am ivory
but what she
really meant was
her style double
since she fancied
my Akubra hat
and the way it
pulled together
my casual rock
t-shirt look
an exact replica
of the look
she hoped to
someday create
and I went home
sensing the presence
of another inside me
who looked at her
face in the mirror
and saw mine

Ocean in a Jar

Two families sharing a cottage at the ocean—
what could go wrong, except for endless rivers of water
that poured from the sky and held the world in suspension
as we waited to see if fishes
would soon appear and we could swim
through the air to catch them in a jar.

As our parents hid in the kitchen and filled jar after jar
with gin, we stared at the ocean,
wishing only to return and swim
again in our ancestral womb of water,
breathing through new sprouted gills like fishes
held in evolutionary suspension.

It was then that I remembered a kind of suspension
for which all you need is paper, pencil, scissors, and a jar.
First, you draw and cut out some fishes
to populate your ocean.
You fill the jar with water,
then shake and twirl to make them swim

and keep it going so they appear to swim
with sufficiently fervent suspension
of disbelief that you come to see the water
swirling round and round in the jar
transfigured into an ocean
of schooling fishes.

Soon everyone wanted their fishes,
spinning their jars to make them swim
in their tiny oceans,
held in fixated suspension
by a simple jar
of water.

Who was that audacious boy who made the water
come to life with swirling fishes
in a pickle jar,
spinning his trick to make them swim?
Was it some magical suspension
of reality to make us all see there an ocean?

I wish that boy with his jar of water
turned to ocean were here to make the fishes
swim again and hold the world in suspension.

The Poet's Job

Watch through the window
to write of things in plain view
like the lone black thong flapping
defiantly in a sea of white briefs.

Listen to the soft tickety sounds
an empty wrapper makes
skimming along the sidewalk
and find there a symphony.

Turn everything into something else.
Code the words obliquely in hopes
someone can tell you what they mean.

Explore dark ovens
and castles of abuse
where muses often lurk.

Feel the earth quaking
and bear witness.

Express the ineffable
with disappearing ink.

Start with one word
and sail the world.

Mourn the spaces
left behind
when there are no words.

Shopping Cart Dreams

They dream of the old days
when a cart's true mettle was
measured by the number of
aisles and parking spaces travelled,
how much it could carry of
premium thread count linens,
plush bath towels for soft tushes,
avocados, chips, and salsa
for the Super Bowl crowd,
computers, big screen TVs
and other Black Friday deals,
colorful wrapped bundles
of Christmas joy,

never dreaming of a future
overflowing with the bedding,
bags, and boxes that hold a life together,
wheeling through endless
streets and alleyways until,
their toils over,
they take one last journey
on worn rubber feet
into the wash by the underpass,
their metal skeletons filled
with the debris of all
they once carried.

About the Author

Gene Twaronite is a Tucson poet and the author of five poetry collections. His first poetry book, *Trash Picker on Mars* (Kelsay Books, 2016), was the winner of a 2017 New Mexico-Arizona Book Award. Other published books include a picture book, novel and collections of essays and short stories. A former Writer-in-Residence for Pima County Public Library, he leads a poetry workshop for the University of Arizona OLLI program.

Follow more of Gene's writing at his website:
genetwaronitepoet.com

www.ingramcontent.com/pod-product-compliance
Lightning Source LLC
Chambersburg PA
CBHW072201160426
43197CB00012B/2478